Table of Contents

Rourke.

Can you find these words?

build

food

ocean

sports

Robots Can

Robots can do many things.

Robots can **build**.
They build cars and trucks.

Robots can build cars faster than people.

Robots can help.
They help put out fires.

Robots help people stay safe.

Robots can make **food.**

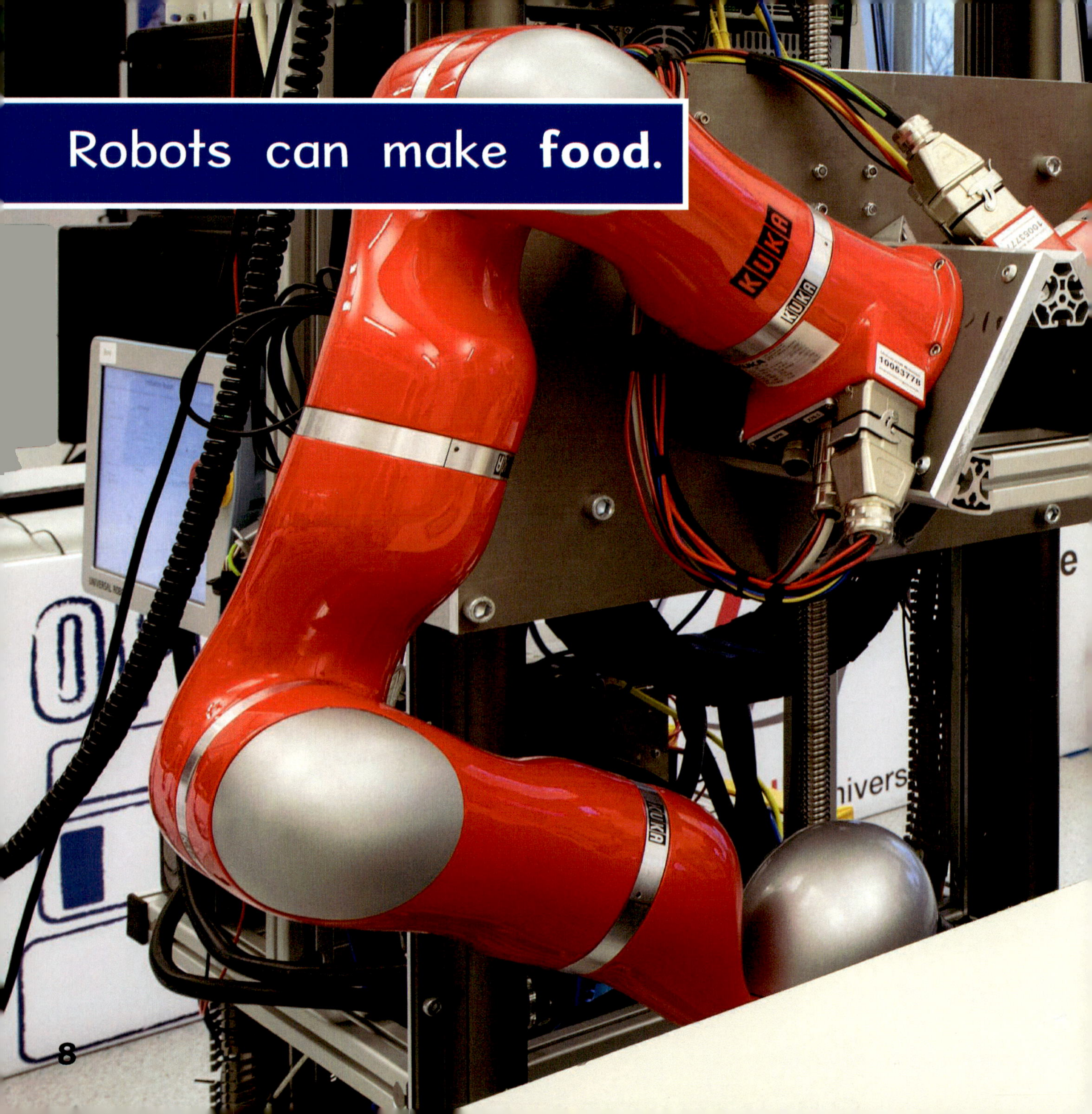

They can make pizza.

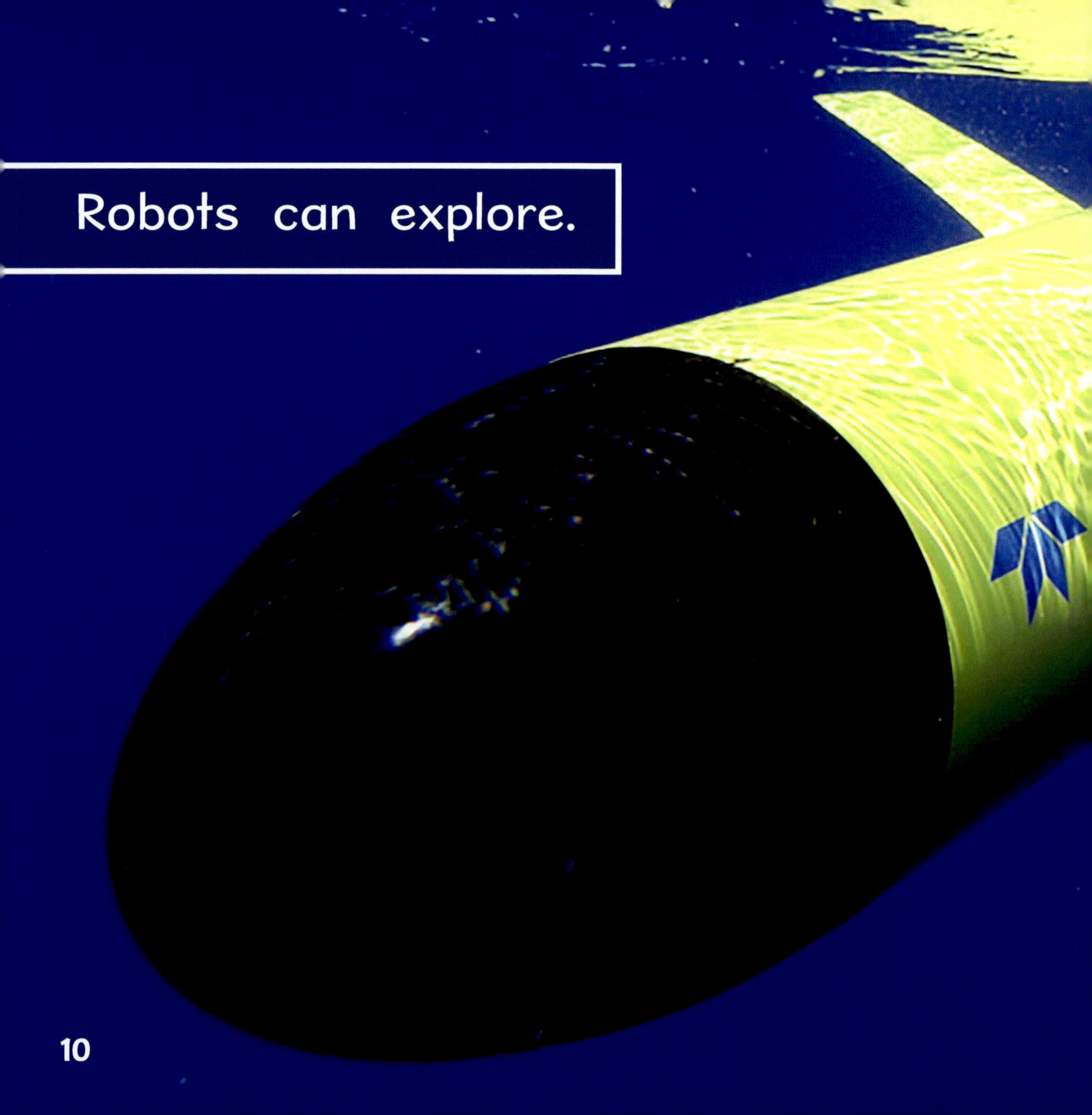

Robots can explore.

They can explore the **ocean**.

Robots can play.
They play music.

They play **sports.**

Did you find these words?

Robots can **build**.

Robots can make **food**.

They can explore the **ocean**.

They play **sports**.

Photo Glossary

build (bild): To make something by putting parts together.

food (food): Things that living creatures eat to stay alive.

ocean (OH-shuhn): A large mass of saltwater.

sports (sports): Games people play that require skill and physical efforts.

Index

About the Author

Charlotte Hunter writes books about everything from friendship to fruit. When she's not writing, she enjoys going for long walks with her dog, Penny.

www.rourkebooks.com

PHOTO CREDITS: Cover: ©NASA; p.2,4-5,14,15: ©shutterstock.com; p.2,8-9,14,15: ©dpa picture alliance/Alamy Stock Photo; p.2,11,14,15: ©IakovKalinin; p.2,13,14,15: ©Richard Wareham Fotografie/Alamy Stock Photo; p.3: ©Ekkasit919; p.6-7: ©Xinhua/Alamy Stock Photo; p.7: ©US Army; p.10-11: ©NOAA; p.12: ©robertharding/Alamy Stock Photo

Edited by: Keli Sipperley
Cover and interior design by: Rhea Magaro-Wallace

Library of Congress PCN Data
Robots Can / Charlotte Hunter
(I Know)
ISBN (hard cover) 978-1-64156-172-3
ISBN (soft cover) 978-164156-228-7
ISBN (e-Book) 978-1-64156-281-2
Library of Congress Control Number: 2017957782

Printed in the United States of America
06-2652511937